TRAUMA

BONDING

Signs And How To

Break Trauma Bonds

Dr, Tiffany J. Bozeman

CONTENT

CHAPTER ONE

Trauma Bonding

Trauma bonding is a sort of connection that can develop between two individuals after they have experienced something terrible or unpleasant together.

Although it may happen in other kinds of relationships as well, it is frequently linked to ones that entail abuse or exploitation.

Even if the connection is destructive and may entail manipulation, coercion, or other types of abuse, the victim of trauma bonding develops an emotional dependence on the abuser.

Despite the repercussions, the victim could feel devoted to the abuser and stay in the relationship.

The bonding that results from trauma can be influenced by a variety of variables. As an illustration, the abuser could manipulate, instill fear in the victim, or exert pressure on them.

The victim could also feel guilty or responsible for the abuser's behavior, or they might think they are stuck in an abusive relationship with no alternative options or sources of support.

It's crucial to be aware of the symptoms of trauma bonding and to get assistance if you're in an unhealthy or abusive relationship.

Breaking the pattern of abuse and reestablishing healthy relationships can be made possible with the aid of professional counseling and support

Trauma Types Bonding

Individuals may experience emotional or psychological suffering as a result of a variety of traumas. Several typical forms of trauma include:

1. Physical trauma: This kind of trauma includes injury or injuries to the body, such as those caused by assault, accidents, or calamities.

2. Emotional trauma: Events or experiences that are overpowering or induce great dread, such as bullying, neglect, or abuse, can result in emotional trauma.

3. Psychological trauma: Situations that put someone's feeling of safety in danger, including war, calamities, or sexual

assault, frequently result in psychological trauma.

4. Complex trauma: Complex trauma is a term for several protracted traumatic events, such as growing up in a violent home or experiencing a protracted war.

5. Developmental trauma: Developmental trauma happens throughout key developmental phases and can have a long-term impact on a person's emotional and psychological health.

It is essential to keep in mind that each person's experience with trauma will be quite distinct and that each person will respond in a unique way to various sorts of trauma.

Additionally, it's crucial to get assistance if you or someone you know is going through trauma because it may seriously harm one's mental health as well as general well-being.

Trauma's Stages And Overlapping

1. Initial attraction: The abuser may be affable and attentive at first, making the victim feel a deep emotional connection to them.

2. The "honeymoon" phase: During this time, the abuser may refrain from their abusive behavior and show kindness to the victim, giving them hope that the violence was an isolated episode and that things would get better.

3. The abuse starts: The abuser could then continue to victimize them, leaving the victim perplexed and unsure of what to do.

4. The pattern of abuse and reconciliation: The abuser may vary between the abusive and reconciling phases, giving the victim reason to

believe that the abuser will eventually change and things will get better. Due to the victim's perception that they are the only ones who can "cure" the abuser, this cycle may result in a close emotional connection between the victim and the abuser.

5. The breaking point: Eventually, the abuse could get so bad or so regular that the victim can't justifiably continue in the relationship.

The victim could then want to end the union and seek support.

Understanding that trauma bonding is a complicated process that may happen in a variety of relationships—including romantic ones, friendships, and even parent-child ones—is vital.

It's crucial to get assistance and support from a dependable friend, relative, or professional if you're in a relationship that contains abuse.

Signs Of Trauma Bonding

Ten indicators of trauma bonding are listed below:

1. Difficulty ending the connection Despite the relationship's negative

effects, you could feel unable or hesitant to end it.

2. Denial of abuse: You might downplay or deny any abuse that had a place in the relationship.

3. Accusing yourself of the abuse: You can think that the abuse was your fault or that you deserved it.

4. A sense of reliance on your abuser: You could believe that you would perish if they left your life and that you depend on them in some way.

5. A strong emotional bond with your abuser despite the pain they have done to you: You could have a deep emotional bond with your abuser.

6. Trouble trusting others: The abuse may have led you to mistrust people or lead you to think that you are unworthy of loving relationships.

7. Poor self-esteem: As a result of the abuse, you may feel unlovable or unworthy of respect, leading to low self-esteem.

8. Difficulty establishing boundaries: The abuse may have led you to feel powerless

over your own life, making it difficult for you to establish and uphold limits in your relationships.

9. A propensity for isolation: To safeguard oneself against more pain, you might shy away from interactions with other people.

10. A feeling of helplessness: If you've been subjected to abuse, you may have lost hope and come to believe that you'll never be able to leave the relationship or find happiness.

It's critical to get support and assistance if you exhibit any of these symptoms. You can use the information to better understand your circumstances and escape the abusive relationship.

Trauma-related Factors Bonding

The following factors may contribute to trauma bonding:

1. Intense emotional encounters: When two individuals have an intense emotional encounter together, such as during a crisis or terrible incident, trauma bonding may take place.

Strong bonds between people might develop as a result of the shared experience.

2. Isolation: People who are cut off from their social network are more prone to form traumatic bonds with manipulative or abusive people.

3. Dependency: A person may be more prone to develop a trauma bond with someone if they are dependent on them for their emotional or physical well-being.

4. Stockholm syndrome: This condition develops when a victim of captivity or

abuse starts to identify with and feel pity for them.

As a result, trauma bonding may occur.

5. Power imbalances: When there is a power imbalance in a relationship, such as when there is abuse or manipulation, trauma bonding can happen.

To manage the other person and uphold the relationship, the individual in a position of more power may employ strategies like gaslighting, emotional manipulation, or coercion.

It's crucial to understand that healthy bonding and attachment are not the same as trauma bonding. It is a harmful pattern that can have detrimental effects on a person's emotional and physical health.

The Best Way To Dissolve A Trauma Bond

1. Seek professional assistance: One of the best ways to break a trauma connection is to work with a therapist or counselor who knows the trauma and abusive relationships.

They may assist you in exploring your emotions, learning how to manage them, and comprehending the complexities of your relationship.

2. Put self-care into action. Your physical and mental health depends on it.

Be sure to get adequate rest, eat healthily, and partake in enjoyable activities.

You'll have a stronger sense of stability and be more equipped to handle the difficulties of severing a trauma attachment as a result.

3. Establish limits: It's crucial to establish precise boundaries with the individual you're attempting to sever ties with.

This entails establishing boundaries for the behaviors you will and will not put up with in the relationship and upholding those boundaries.

4. Cut off contact: Depending on the level of abuse, it could be necessary to stop communicating with the individual you are attempting to sever your link with.

Although it might be challenging, doing this is frequently required for your security and well-being.

5. Seek support: Having a network of friends, family, or a support group can be beneficial while you work through the

process of severing a trauma attachment. It may make a great difference to have somebody you can talk to and depend on.

It may take some time and effort to successfully break a trauma link.

However, it is possible to leave an unhealthy and violent relationship and go ahead to a better and happier future with the correct help and tools.

Trauma bonding may have negative, protracted impacts. Because they have grown emotionally attached to their abuser and may think they can influence their abuser's behavior, victims of trauma bonding may find it difficult to leave an abusive relationship.

In addition, individuals could feel devotion to their abuser and worry about punishment if they try to escape.

The emotional and psychological impacts of trauma bonding might include melancholy, anxiety, low self-esteem, and post-traumatic stress disorder (PTSD). They could also suffer from self-blame and feelings of worthlessness.

For trauma-bonding victims to end the cycle of abuse and recover from the psychological repercussions of the trauma, they must reach out for support and assistance.

This may entail going to counseling, participating in support groups, and asking trustworthy friends and family members for assistance.

Note

Relationship formation and maintenance are both significantly impacted by trauma. Trauma survivors may find it difficult to connect with people or may have a mistaken idea of what a good relationship looks like.

For instance, a traumatized person may be more prone to codependent relationships, where they feel compelled to continuously put their partner's needs before their own. Additionally, they could have a hard time building close, personal connections and trouble with trust.

On the other side, someone who has gone through trauma could also have an avoidant attachment style, where they keep their distance from other people and struggle to build strong, personal bonds.

It's crucial to remember that everyone experiences trauma differently, and how it affects a person's relationships depends on their unique circumstances and recovery processes. In addition, it's critical to understand that with the correct resources and assistance, individuals who have endured trauma may create wholesome, happy relationships.